Flee the Dra

Negotiating when all els

Flee the Dragon

Negotiating when all else fails

Leonie McKeon

DoctorZed
Publishing
www.doctorzed.com

Books may be ordered through booksellers or by contacting:
www.leoniemckeon.com

1st edition published by DoctorZed Publishing
www.doctorzed.com

ISBN: 978-0-6485361-3-0 (hc)
ISBN: 978-0-6485361-4-7 (sc)
ISBN: 978-0-6485361-5-4 (ebk)

A CiP number for this title can be found at the National Library of Australia.

Cover image © Trish Pollock

Printed in Australia, UK and USA.
rev. date 30/05/2021

Contents

Acknowledgements

I am finally at the conclusion of the series *The Dao of Negotiation: The Path between Eastern Strategies and Western Minds*. Writing the six books that comprise the complete series has been a long journey, and I have learnt a great deal about authorship.

No one writes even a single book without a lot of help and support from a wide circle of people. Writing six books has meant that my circle of helpers and supporters has been very wide. As always, I want to thank my publisher, Dr. Scott Zarcinas at DoctorZed Publishing, editor Hari Teah, and designer Trish Pollock at BrandArk, whose skills have contributed so much to these books. Additionally, I would like to give a big thanks to Nicole Turner for teaching me how to write and design the content.

Thank you to Melpomene (Mellie) Tantalos for her wonderful research skills and contributions to this final book *Flee the Dragon: Negotiating when all else fails*, and special thanks to the other five excellent research assistants, without whom creating this series would have been so much harder. They are Michaela Crisp, Cassandra Heffernan, Carla Morelli, Kate Lyall, and Suzanne McKenzie.

In addition to reading endless drafts, my sister Jennifer McKeon has remained continuously optimistic in relation to the entire *The Dao of Negotiation: The Path between Eastern Strategies and Western Minds* series of books.

Last, and in no way least, my heartfelt thanks go to Shelley Rogers, who has used her skills in organisational psychology to help me think through the intricacies of each story and the most relevant examples to accompany them. Shelley has been consistent in her support for me and for the *The Dao of Negotiation* project, for which I am endlessly appreciative.

"The supreme art of war is to subdue the enemy without fighting."

Sun Tzu, *The Art of War*

Leonie's Journey Reaches a Conclusion

*M*y experiences during my China journey have led me in many directions. The most significant road has been developing my understanding of the application of the 36 Strategies. Book Six - *Flee the Dragon: Negotiating when all else fails,* is the final book completing the six-book series *The Dao of Negotiation: The Path between Eastern strategies and Western minds.* During my writing I have discovered that the 36 Strategies can be used in any negotiating environment. In each book, I demonstrate examples of how these strategies can be used in a Western environment, as well as when working with Chinese people. This realisation was huge as it became apparent to me that in Western business culture, we do not have a rich or complex framework within which to negotiate. *The Dao of Negotiation: The Path between Eastern strategies and Western minds* fills this gap.

I continue to work with Western businesses that are engaging with China and the Greater China Region. I am also working with Western businesses to assist them to understand the application of the 36 Strategies in an entirely Western context. Each book in *The Dao of Negotiation: The Path between Eastern strategies and Western minds* series stands alone and can be read separately without reference to the other books. The 36 Strategies themselves flow in a sequence. Book One - *Tame the Tiger: Negotiating from a position of power*, discusses the Advantageous Strategies and the meaning of *Dao*. Book Two - *Deceive the Dragon: Negotiating to retain power*, talks about the Opportunistic Strategies. In Book Two I also discuss *guanxi*. Book Three - *Lure the Tiger: Negotiating in confronting circumstances*, provides scenarios for the Strategies for Attack, and describes 'face'. Book Four - *Bewilder the Dragon: Negotiating amongst confusion* provides examples for the Confusion Strategies and discusses Confucianism and how this ideology is very relevant in the contemporary Chinese business world. In Book Five - *Endure the Tiger: Negotiating to gain ground,* I discuss the Strategies for Gaining Ground and I describe the Pinyin system. In Book Six - *Flee the Dragon: Negotiating when all else fails,* I describe the Strategies for Desperate Situations and discuss hierarchy, which is very relevant in the Chinese business environment.

Even though the 36 Strategies are 2,500 years old, they are timeless. Learning how to recognise and apply each of the 36 Strategies with Chinese people from the Greater China Region and in any Western business environment, will be one of the most significant and best investments you will ever make.

Hierarchy

Chinese society is hierarchical, which means respect is focused on people who occupy positions of a higher status within the Chinese social structure. The concept of hierarchy is heavily influenced by Confucianism. As we have explored in Book Four – *Bewilder the Dragon: Negotiating amongst confusion*, Confucianism relates to the relationships: between parent and child, elder and younger siblings, husband and wife, elder and junior friends, and ruler and subject.

In a business context, this emphasis on hierarchical relationships manifests in several ways. All employees are expected to show respect for one another, and to accept the obligations and duties that come with their position in their hierarchical structure. Younger employees are required to show respect to their older co-workers and business associates.

Hierarchy is apparent in a Chinese banquet business setting. Guests are seated according to their relationship with the host of the banquet; therefore, guests need to wait to be seated. If you are the host, you arrive before your guests and have everything ready by the time they arrive. If you and your guests are going to the restaurant together, you must allow your guests to walk through the doorway first. When ordering food guests always let the host do the ordering.

It is important when toasting that you toast a specific person. Then you stand up, holding your glass in both hands, with the rim of your glass touching below the rim of the glass of the person whom you are toasting. This demonstrates humbleness and respect. On the other hand, if you are of a higher status, you do not need to lower your glass.

To communicate effectively with a Chinese person and understand their mindset and therefore the way they behave, it is crucial to understand hierarchy. These hierarchical elements of social interaction within Chinese society are reflected in the ways people communicate and behave. The hierarchy of the Chinese people with whom you are dealing will determine how you address them, where you sit in the meeting room, and how you introduce your group. Therefore, it is very important to understand the hierarchy of the Chinese people with whom you are meeting and negotiating.

Strategies for Desperate Situations

These final six strategies, which are Strategies 31 - 36, are **Strategies for Desperate Situations.** They are used in situations where the strategist is significantly weaker than their opponent, and where the likelihood of not meeting their objective is high. The most effective time to use these strategies is when the strategist has limited resources, and they want to produce the greatest gain for the smallest investment.

The aim of the strategist is to confuse or outsmart their opponent, and so the correct execution of these strategies is critical. When the stakes are high, these strategies are often the most difficult of the strategies to execute, because even a small mistake could lead to a serious loss. When applying this group of strategies, flexibility is extremely important. It is also crucial to understand all the 36 Strategies well, because it is likely that the strategist will have to use several of the other strategies for the successful application of Strategies 31 - 36.

Strategies for
Desperate Situations

The strategy of beautiful women means *"to use their passions to get them to drop their guard"*

Send your enemy beautiful women to cause discord within his camp.

During the warring times in China, the states of Wu and Yue were constantly fighting over ownership of territory. Fu Chai, the king of Wu, was a famous king, and because of his fame he was extremely unapproachable. He continually surrounded himself with a large entourage who guarded him closely. His security guard organised this entourage.

Fan Li was a clever strategist for the state of Yue and held the position of a high-level key advisor. He decided to apply Strategy Thirty-One – **The strategy of beautiful women**. To use this strategy, he '*caused discord within the Fu Chai court*'. He researched what Fu Chai was interested in. His findings revealed that he liked visual and performing arts and was also fascinated by the perfection of beautiful women.

Fan Li found Xi Shi who was known for her beauty. He sent her to a prestigious dancing school, and also had her educated in reciting poetry and painting beautiful pictures. Xi Shi's job was to recite poetry, paint pictures, and dance for Fu Chai. She also had to learn information about the kingdom to report this back to Fan Li. Xi Shi had many long conversations with Fu Chai, and was able to extract important information about the kingdom from him.

Fan Li instructed Xi Shi to convince Fu Chai that neither his head bodyguard nor his senior advisor could be trusted. Fu Chai was so mesmerised by Xi Shi's beauty and her wonderful talents that he soon lost interest in running his kingdom which resulted in him missing many important meetings, and he quickly began losing trust in his bodyguard and his advisor.

This loss of trust quickly accelerated because Xi Shi told him that his advisor was pestering him to go to the meetings in order to control how he spent his time. Xi Shi also convinced Fu Chai that his advisor was jealous Fu Chai was enjoying the visual and performing arts Xi Shi provided. She told Fu Chai that his advisor was planning to have him murdered, and that this meant attending the meetings was very dangerous. As he placed so much trust in Xi Shi, he believed what she said, and told his head bodyguard and senior advisor to leave their positions, ordering them to work far away from the main political arena of the kingdom. This meant he was left with little protection.

Knowing Fu Chai now had no organised protection, Fan Li ordered his army to attack and kill Fu Chai, leaving the state of Wu without a king. Strategy Thirty-One was applied successfully and Fan Li was able to conquer the kingdom of Wu. Prior to taking over the kingdom of Wu he had a lot of knowledge about the workings of the kingdom, which Xi Shi had relayed to him. This information made taking over the kingdom very easy.

The successful application of Strategy Thirty-One requires conducting extensive research to find something that is attractive to your opponent, and then using this to get close to them in order to gain information. This information will then be of an advantage to future business objectives.

Negotiating with Chinese People

EXAMPLE ONE
Strategy Thirty- One in action (against you)

In this scenario, you have developed a unique engineering product which has taken five years of hard work. The product has a digital application that can be used for elderly people to detect immediate health issues. In your own country there is a Chinese company interested in exporting your product to China. Their office is conveniently located, because they are close in proximity to where you have your business.

The Chinese company has approached you to talk about possibly licensing the intellectual property of your product, which is great news for you. They plan to host you and your senior team members at a Chinese banquet in a very reputable restaurant. To gather information about your product, they cleverly apply Strategy Thirty-One. At the time they plan to pick you up, you have another meeting. However, you have organised to meet them at the restaurant. You inform them that your most senior manager would be delighted to show them around the office and be escorted to the restaurant. Your senior manager has an obsession for BMW cars, which they revealed through their social media.

The Chinese group researched this, and are aware of your senior manager's obsession.

They drove to your office in the latest model BMW, which your senior manager was infatuated with. It was when your senior manager was travelling in the BMW that they were able to '*cause discord within your company*'. The Chinese group had a glass of champagne waiting for your senior manager and the Chinese group's senior staff member sat in the back seat of the BMW and talked with your senior manager. Things seemed to be going well, and by this stage your senior manager was captivated with the opulence of the surroundings. Your senior manager had a lot of input into the design of this intellectual property and was very excited about the prospect of being able to talk about the product. In fact, they did not stop talking about this product until they arrived at the restaurant.

To apply Strategy Thirty-One, the Chinese senior manager asked many questions. During this conversation there were things that the Western senior manager should not have discussed because they were disclosing confidential information. The Chinese company should have purchased the intellectual property before such things were disclosed about the product. Armed with this information, the Chinese company could go to another company to ask about the design of something similar in the hope of securing the same basic product at a much cheaper price. When the BMW arrived at the restaurant with your senior manager the Chinese group went to the private room, leaving your group in the foyer. You saw that your senior manager was very excited that they had been driven to the restaurant in their favourite model BMW, while drinking expensive champagne and talking about their involvement in the product. The Chinese group let you wait in the foyer for about fifteen minutes. Unbeknown to you they were discussing what your senior manager had told them on the way to the restaurant.

You were called into the private restaurant room and guided to your seat. When you began discussions, you realised that the Chinese group knew a lot about your product and had therefore placed themselves in the position of having a lot more bargaining power. It became apparent that they had enough knowledge to go to another company and get a similar product made. They had successfully applied Strategy Thirty-One because they researched what your senior manager was interested in, which led them to talking with your senior manager and extracting critical information about the product, then reporting this back to the head person in their company before the dinner.

Being knowledgeable about the intricacies of the intellectual property meant they were able to negotiate a much cheaper price than you had anticipated. You knew if you did not accept this price, they could now go somewhere else to have the product made. If you let this happen it would be disastrous for your business because the situation would have established a competitor, which you did not want. The best decision was to accept the lower price.

Example One
Guarding yourself against Strategy Thirty-One

When Strategy Thirty-One is applied it is crucial to understand to whom it may be applied, and what weaknesses this may be used on. In this situation it was used on the most senior staff member who was seriously involved in the design of the product. As this person was excited about the idea of their product being licensed by a Chinese company, they could not resist sharing information about the product. Preparation about what the Chinese company were likely to discuss while travelling to the restaurant would have been useful. To discuss things openly was obviously a personal quality of this senior staff member, and it may have been more beneficial to send someone who was unlikely to act in this way, but rather to send someone who keeps their cards close to their chest. Be aware that Chinese business people will go to great lengths to apply a strategy or strategies in an organised manner, to achieve a favourable outcome.

In Chinese business meetings, even though they may take place at glamorous restaurants or in luxurious cars, remember that everything has a purpose. This kind of environment can be quite seductive, so it is important to be careful what you say. Once the information is given in an unguarded manner, it is likely to be reported to a higher authority and then used to get a better deal. Although it is important to be friendly, always be careful what you say and how much information you are disclosing. Western staff need to be trained to communicate appropriately with Chinese business people without offering too much information.

EXAMPLE TWO
Strategy Thirty-One in action (against you)

You are connected with some entrepreneurial Chinese contacts who are interested in seeing your unique solar energy technology. You are a leader in your field within your country and are very keen to expand into China. You have been invited by these Chinese contacts to introduce them to your technology. Conveniently, the Chinese company is in a city that is just one hour by plane from you. You arrive in their city and they collect you from the airport, and the first thing they want to do is take you to their office, which is over an hour's drive from the airport. Initially, you were concerned about their limited English, as you did not believe it was good enough to have a detailed business discussion. However, you thought that you would just go with the flow because you perceived this to be an exploratory meeting. Your plan was that if everything worked out in this first meeting you would return to their office for a meeting accompanied by an interpreter.

When you were picked up at the airport, much to your surprise, the person who met you was a Western person who also spoke very good Chinese. You felt relieved; however, what you did not realise was that the Chinese company were applying Strategy Thirty-One. They were sending their equivalent of a '*beautiful woman*' – in this instance a Western man with whom you could converse, and therefore there would be no communication issues. This situation made you feel comfortable, so much so that you felt fine about discussing your product in detail.

During the drive to their offices, they asked many questions about your product, which included price, the lifecycle of the product, and the location that you were interested in exporting to. The person communicating with you was very friendly, and because you did not understand the 36 Strategies you perceived no need to guard against discussing your product. What you did not realise was that this was a strategy to extract information from you. The person who picked you up at the airport had been hired specifically to act as a key component in the application of Strategy Thirty-One. When you arrived at the Chinese company's offices, the Western business person took you into the offices and sat you in the boardroom.

You were given Chinese tea, and after several minutes a team of four people entered the boardroom, all of whom were all Chinese business people with limited English. There was no Western business person to be found. Although their English was very limited, they had been prepared for the meeting by being given the information you discussed in the car on the way to their office. From this information they already knew the price of your product, and they offered you a price that was much lower than you anticipated. This left you in a no-win situation, because they were already familiar with your price and other related issues about your product. The result was you accepting this lower price because you were keen to enter the China market. Strategy Thirty-One had been successfully applied on you, and unfortunately you have come out of this situation with less financial benefit than you had planned.

EXAMPLE TWO
Guarding yourself against Strategy Thirty-One

To be a leader in your field in your own country is a big achievement. However, you need to keep in mind that when you are dealing with China you must initially establish your reputation, as they do not know you. It can often take many interactions to build a solid relationship before you even begin to create a strong reputation. Then your product needs to be consumed in China to gain credibility. In this situation you needed to think through the implications of being picked up at the airport, because when this happened you essentially gave up control.

Even though you are passionate about talking about your product, it is important to be careful what you say. In the Chinese business environment negotiations will commence the minute you encounter the Chinese company, whereas in Western culture, business generally commences in the boardroom. The Chinese group were aware that providing someone you could converse with would make you feel comfortable.

When meeting with Chinese business people, act on the premise that there is a purpose behind every action. Do not just move into a conversation where you are freely answering all the questions. Always remember you are dealing with expert negotiators. It would have been a clever business move to tell them you had another commitment. In this way, you would be able to find your own way to their office rather than having them pick you up from the airport. You could have gone to your hotel, checked in, and then organised your own transport to their offices. This would have given you some control over the situation. If there is no opportunity to do this and you are being picked up by the Chinese group, it is not wise to discuss details such as price. If you find yourself in a place where you must discuss price do not tell Chinese business people your bottom line, rather you always need to start much higher. Take every interaction connected with this meeting seriously. When you feel as though you can relax because you can clearly converse with them, think of this as a dangerous place, because you may feel comfortable enough to disclose critical information.

Learning a few key words and phrases in Mandarin Chinese is a good idea, because this would give you confidence. For this you can go to **www.pronouncemandarin.com**. Learning about the 36 Strategies is necessary, so that you know what is being played out. The most important thing is to think through the scenario and make sure you are not in a position where you are disclosing information that will be used against you in the negotiation.

Key Points when Strategy Thirty-One is used against you

- Understand your weaknesses, strengths, and desires.
- When you are feeling safe during a business negotiation, you may be at risk.
- Your emotional desires can be weaknesses that cause you to let your guard down.

Example Three
Enacting Strategy Thirty-One

You are an up and coming architect who recently commenced a new position. This position is in a different city from where you formerly resided and studied for your university degree. You have been living and working in this new city for one year. The position is with a reputable Chinese architectural firm. One year has been sufficient time to get to know the culture of the workplace. You have befriended an employee in the company who is near retirement age and who is originally from China. His family have taken you into their home, almost like their own family member. You go to their home regularly for some wonderful Chinese meals, and you enjoy the family's welcoming hospitality.

At the firm, there is a project to design a new state-of-the-art hotel in the city. You want to be a part of this project and are confident you have the skills. However, you do not know what is required for you to be accepted onto the project team. You also do not know much about dealing with Chinese business culture. Applications to be part of this project team are open. The person that you have befriended is good friends with the project manager and has worked with them on several projects. Your friend knows that the person who manages this important project really likes a particular fish restaurant close to the offices. In this situation you can apply Strategy Thirty-One by sending your friend to talk with the person who manages the project to find out what is required to successfully apply for a place on the project team. When your work colleague took the project manager out for a meal to their favourite restaurant, they enquired about the requirements of the project. Your friend relayed this information about the project back to you, and you then were able to write an application that targeted the exact requirements of the project. You are thrilled, because your application was successful.

By applying Strategy Thirty-One you have been able to fast-track your position within the company. Even before the application of Strategy Thirty-One you were confident that you had the skills to be a part of this project. Even so, you had no way of knowing whether the information you were submitting was what they wanted. After finding out what they required, you were able to meet the needs of the application. Following the hotel project, you were invited to be part of other large state-of-the-art projects.

Negotiating in a Western Environment

EXAMPLE FOUR
Enacting Strategy Thirty-One

Imagine you are writing a tender for a large project which has the potential to advance your career. It is important to you that your proposal is sufficiently competitive to win against the other firms that are bidding for the contract. You have read the tender invitation carefully and researched the client's organisation in detail. In spite of this, you feel that gaining more information may give you an edge over your competitors.

To gather more information about the tender application you apply Strategy Thirty-One to help you achieve your goal. Applying Strategy Thirty-One means you need to search for a person in your network who can act as your '*beautiful woman*'. This person will be the person that you intend to use to extract information from a reliable source. You search for someone who has access to a person connected enough to be able to gather information on your behalf. This information will then help you provide the right content for the tender application.

To see if you can find any connections to the client within your networks, you search the potential client's organisational charts and recognise a familiar name. You recall that a friend of yours once worked with this person and talked about this person frequently. You call your friend to see if they are still in touch with this person, and whether they are willing to engage with them in a casual meeting to extract some of the information you need. Your friend confirms that they are regularly in touch with this person and would be happy to arrange a meeting with them. Your friend knows this person enjoys going to a particular coffee shop. They arrange to take them there after work and treat them to their favourite coffee. During this meeting, your friend asks several questions about the people assessing the tender applications, and the project in question. After the meeting they pass this important information to you.

You now have some additional information, which is likely to give you the edge you needed to win the tender. The information includes details about the specific people assessing the tenders, such as whether they prefer emotive language referencing the company's values or straight-to-the-point business talk; expectations around the level of detail in your tender, such as whether a thorough 40-page report or a concise 10-page report is desired; and project priorities, such as whether it is more important to deliver within a tight timeframe, or within a tight budget. The more information you have, the better you can tailor your tender to resonate with the client's needs, and therefore the better chance you have of winning the contract.

Key Points when using Strategy Thirty-One

- Use a reliable third party to gather information you require.
- Employ others to help you access the information that you seek.
- The 'beautiful woman' can be anyone who engages and is appreciated by your target.

The strategy of open city gates means *"to do the unexpected to confuse your opponent"*

When the enemy is superior in numbers and your situation is such that you expect to be overrun at any moment, then drop all pretence of military preparedness and act casually. Unless the enemy has an accurate description of your situation, this unusual behaviour will arouse suspicions. With luck, he will be dissuaded from attacking.

*J*n 149 B.C, in the three-kingdoms period, Wang Min, the leader of the state of Shu, planned to attack the state of Wei. The Wei army was led by general Si Ma. Wang Min was a very strategic leader and planned his attack carefully. He sent 50,000 soldiers in advance of this attack. The two sides, both with 50,000 troops each, fought the battle. In this instance, the Wei side were particularly good soldiers. After the Shu army were defeated, the Wei army quickly turned on the rest of Wang Min's group.

At this point Wang Min began the application of Strategy Thirty-Two – The strategy of open city gates. He applied this strategy because the Wei army '*was superior in numbers and their situation was such that they expected to be overrun at any moment*'. The situation was critical because the Shu army could not outrun the Wei army. When they arrived at the Shu city of Yangping, Wang Min knew that his army were outnumbered, and therefore they were likely to be defeated.

As a last resort he applied Strategy Thirty-Two, by '*dropping all pretence of military preparedness and acting casually*'. To do this he dressed his army in civilian clothes and sent an elderly man to open the city gates. Wang Min positioned himself in a tower and began to recite poetry and play his flute while his servants brought him food and wine. The idea was that '*this unusual behaviour would arouse suspicions*'.

General Si Ma of the Wei army arrived at Yangping and witnessed what he felt was a peculiar scene. He became suspicious, which is exactly what Wang Min had planned. His thought was that this situation seemed very strange and unusual, and therefore must be a trap. Having this feeling '*he was dissuaded from attacking*'. He ordered his men to retreat from fighting the Shu army, and left the city of Yangping,

Strategy Thirty-Two is a desperate strategy where the only way out of a situation is to do something completely unexpected in the hope that this behaviour arouses suspicion and doubts in your opponent.

Negotiating with Chinese People

EXAMPLE ONE
Strategy Thirty-Two in action (against you)

In this situation you have a very upmarket product, and you are the leaders in your field in your own country. You manufacture umbrellas that are mostly used for sun protection. Even before sun protection was an issue in

Western countries, Chinese people were using umbrellas to guard them from the sun. Traditionally, this has been because they have wanted to keep their skin as fair as possible.

Over the last year you have developed a very strong relationship with someone you consider to be a reputable Chinese business partner. Additionally, your local government office has assisted you with a distributor in China. Feeling confident in your product, you take charge and communicate with this distributor yourself, not realising that you would have been wise to give your Chinese business partner some power in this.

Over the last six months you have discussed many aspects of the manufacturing and production of your umbrellas with your Chinese business partner. As you have gone alone and organised a large deal with the distributor in China, this has caused 'loss of face' to your Chinese business partner. 'Face', which is how you are seen in front of other people, is explained in Book Three – *Lure the Tiger: Negotiating in confronting circumstances*. In the meantime, before this deal has been finalised with the distributor, your Chinese business partner has researched other foreign brands to partner with. Unfortunately, the 'loss of face' has been so devastating for your Chinese business partner that they no longer want to work with you.

To extract themselves from this partnership they applied Strategy Thirty-Two. Not understanding what was going on, you took control because you were '*superior and they were overrun*'. To break ties with you '*they acted in an unusual way*'. They did not want to tell you how they felt because this interaction would have added to their 'loss of face'. This unusual behaviour was to '*dissuade you from wanting to deal with them*'. For the next few meetings, they displayed very odd behaviour. They would normally want to go to a restaurant after a meeting. However, after this situation they would just leave the office without wanting to engage in any informal activities.

This behaviour went on for several weeks to the point where you felt nervous and you decided to dissolve the partnership agreement. They partnered with another Western company, which gave them much more control in the context of communicating with their distributor, and therefore enabled them to feel they were more trusted by their Western business partners. The successful application of Strategy Thirty-Two left you without an appropriate Chinese business partner.

Example One
Guarding yourself against Strategy Thirty-Two

It would have been advisable to learn about the 36 Strategies and the concept of 'face', so the behaviour that caused 'loss of face' could have been avoided. Having the confidence to take control is good. However, this 'go it alone' attitude caused a 'loss of face'. To build up trust it would have been good business practice to allow your Chinese business partner to have some communication with the Chinese distributor. When the Chinese business partner started to act differently it was not a good idea to simply dissolve the partnership, rather look at why their behaviour had changed. In this case the 'loss of face' caused this behaviour, and therefore they wanted to get out of this partnership without direct confrontation. An analysis of the behaviour through a Chinese cultural perspective would have been useful.

The Chinese business partner was left out of the picture regarding the meeting with the local government officials and therefore felt pushed aside and unimportant. As Chinese business people generally use an indirect approach, they applied Strategy Thirty-Two to exit the business partnership. Even though they may have been happy dealing with a highly sought-after export product, 'face' is imbedded in Chinese culture. Therefore the 'loss of face' overtook wanting to stay in a partnership where they had no control and little input into the decision-making. Once they had 'lost face' and decided to exit from the business deal, the application of Strategy Thirty-Two was the best way for them to do this. During the time of applying Strategy Thirty-Two the Chinese business partner was in the process of researching another potential Western business partner. This could have been avoided with more intuition and understanding of the humiliation that 'loss of face' can cause a Chinese business person.

EXAMPLE TWO
Strategy Thirty-Two in action (against you)

In this scenario you want to import high-quality computer cases and other business luggage. Your company is quite large and well-known. To make connections and see what is available in China you attend an exhibition that specialises in business luggage in Shanghai. On your first day at the exhibition, you gather costings and collect brochures from the exhibitors. Even though most of your conversations at the exhibition are through an interpreter, this is what you expected because you do not speak any Chinese.

In the first instance, the quantity that you want to purchase is not large because you want to try the products before you purchase a large order. There is one company at the exhibition who stands out, as they have excellent quality products and a good reputation in the field of exporting their goods to foreign countries. You talk with the other exhibitors, although you do not talk about serious business because you are focused on the one company with the high-quality products you require.

On the second day you approach the company that you are most impressed with. When approaching their stand, you explained to them that you only require a small order so you can see what you think of their products before making a larger order. The order is extremely small, almost to the point where it could be described as a sample. These exhibitors had other customers visit their stand at the same time you were there. The potential customers implied that they wanted to purchase a large order. To focus their attention on these customers they applied Strategy Thirty-Two. They '*dropped all pretence of preparedness and acted casually*' by inviting you into their exhibition stand and, even though they were friendly, they focused on the deficiencies of their products.

This was confusing for you, and you had no idea they were applying Strategy Thirty-Two. The other potential clients at their stand may not have the reputation your company has. Even so, they were talking about placing very large orders. When you informed them about the very small order you wanted to place, they did not want you at their stand because they saw you as a time waster, and therefore chose to spend the time with a client who was potentially going to place a much larger order. By applying Strategy Thirty-Two, '*their behaviour dissuaded you from staying at the stand*'. They continued to inform you about their product deficits, which eventually drove you to leave their stand.

You realised the other people at their stand were treated very differently to you. This was evident when you heard them talk to these people about the advantages of their products as opposed to the deficiencies. It then became obvious to you that your order was far too small for them to want you as a customer, especially when they had customers at their stand who wanted to place a much larger order. By not understanding how Strategy Thirty-Two is applied, you lost the opportunity to buy from this high-quality company. The only option was to revisit the other exhibition stands, where you could place a small order. However, these other companies did not have a wide product range and the quality was of a lower standard. These other companies also had less experience in the international market.

Example Two
Guarding yourself against Strategy Thirty-Two

Attending an exhibition in China is a great idea because you can research products you may want to import. This method of research means you gain knowledge of the available choice of products. However, before attending an exhibition it is a good idea to understand something about how the 36 Strategies are applied and to have some basics in Mandarin Chinese. An excellent way to learn this is to go to **www.pronouncemandarin.com**. This provides a simple way to learn how to pronounce Chinese names and teaches you some key Mandarin Chinese words and phrases.

Choosing one company that you are interested in may be risky, because if that company does not work out you have no other company to import products from. Having at least two or even three alternatives is a good idea. When communicating with the company that you felt was the best one for you, it was not a good idea to initially reveal to them that you only wanted a very small amount of their products. As a visitor to an exhibition, a 'watch and see' attitude is useful. In the situation where there were other customers at the stand you could have waited until they left. If these other customers wanted a large order and you wanted to talk with the people at the exhibition stand, it is highly likely that they will apply Strategy Thirty-Two on you because they will be more interested in dealing with the larger clients. It is important to choose the right moment to introduce yourself and choose what you say.

Key Points when Strategy Thirty-Two is used against you

- If your business contact is behaving strangely, try to understand why this is happening, do not just walk away.
- 'Face' is so critical in Chinese culture that causing 'loss of face' might be enough to end a business relationship.
- Watch and wait for the right time to speak with your Chinese contact at an exhibition.

EXAMPLE THREE
Enacting Strategy Thirty-Two

In this scenario you are a real estate agent, and you have a house to sell that you know will be very attractive to potential Chinese customers. The reason for this house being attractive to potential Chinese customers is because it is Number Eight in the street and eight is an auspicious number in Chinese culture. You have already sold the house next door to a Chinese family, at Number Ten. The Chinese family from Number Ten have been very happy with your service thus far. During the open inspection at Number Eight, there have been quite a few Chinese families who have shown considerable interest.

There is one Chinese family who is extremely interested in purchasing the house. They have enough funds to pay for the house without having to raise any finance. In fact, because the house is Number Eight, they probably would not even question having to pay more for the house than it is worth. This is a slightly tricky situation, because the people who live at Number Ten also have some close relatives interested in buying Number Eight. In this situation you really want to sell this house to Number Ten's family members. You not only have a good relationship with the people in Number Ten, they also have several other relatives who are interested in using your services. The best way for you to succeed and achieve the outcome you want is to apply Strategy Thirty-Two.

To do this, instead of trying to sell the house to the affluent family by stating all the positives of the house '*you drop all pretence and act casually*'. You tell them about the things that the house does not have, which *'will dissuade them from wanting to buy the house'*. You focus on the negative aspects of the location, such as the fact that it is not within walking distance of a shopping centre. From several discussions you find out that their parents will be living in the house with them. You explain that the nearest aged care facility is a fifteen-minute drive from the property. They are aware that at some point their parents may have to live in an aged care home, and therefore this location is not likely to be of interest to them because the aged care facility is too far away. After hearing what you have to say about the house, they are no longer interested in purchasing Number Eight.

To meet their needs, you refer them to one of your respected colleagues who can locate a house that is more suited to their overall requirements. You sell the house to Number Ten's relatives, who are very happy with their purchase. You also get several other Chinese clients from the people at Number Ten. From successfully thinking this through and applying Strategy Thirty-Two you have satisfied the people you sold the house to and you have also met the needs of the people you did not sell the house to, while still getting the desired price.

Negotiating in a Western Environment

EXAMPLE FOUR
Enacting Strategy Thirty-Two

In this scenario you are the owner of a small furniture store, situated in a shopping precinct on a main road. Your rent has recently increased, and you are frustrated with some of the disadvantages of being in this strip of shops. You have just found out that a boutique competitor, who compared to you, *'is superior'* in this market, is looking to rent the vacant shop next to yours. If they rent this shop *'you expect to be overrun at any time'* and this could significantly damage your business. Even though there are disadvantages for you in this area, it would cost you more to move so you want to focus on building the business and not having to relocate.

To overcome this situation, you apply Strategy Thirty-Two on your potential business neighbours. You research your competitor and find out they are quite successful, but not local. In fact, this will be their first business venture in this geographical location. Their products are upmarket, and more expensive than your products. They are a well-known company and have the resources to spend considerable funds on advertising. They are still in the early stages of their negotiation with the property agent and are now interested in learning more about the other shops in the precinct.

When the prospective new store owner visits your store you *'drop all pretences of preparedness and act casually'*. You invite them to your shop for a cup of coffee and casually discuss their future plans. You act extremely friendly, happy-go-lucky, and relaxed, showing no indication of anxiety relating to the fact that they may be moving in next door to you. You decide to expose the absolute truth regarding the circumstances of the area, by telling them about the recent increase in rent, the difficult landlord, the ridiculously high council rates, and parking rules which prevent potential customers from parking on the road outside the store. You reveal that the trucks which transport furniture do not fit comfortably in the loading dock, and you must unload stock on the main road.

When your competitor hears about these difficulties, they decide not to move to your area. They have been *'dissuaded from moving next door to your shop.'*

Key Points when using Strategy Thirty-Two

- To build solid relationships, take the time to keep all parties happy.
- Focus on what is important for your competitors.
- Extensively research so you really understand your customers' and competitors' needs.

Strategy Thirty-Three

The strategy of sowing discord means *"to provide inaccurate information to mislead your opponent, especially through informal channels"*

Undermine your enemy's ability to fight by secretly causing discord between him and his friends, allies, advisors, family, commanders, soldiers, and population. While he is preoccupied settling internal disputes, his ability to attack or defend is compromised.

The warlord of Wei, Cao Cao was on a mission to defeat Zhou Yu, who was the general of Wu. As Cao Cao's army's strength was to fight on dry land, during the previous battles he was forced into marshland and defeated every time. On the other hand, Zhou Yu was trained in naval combat and was therefore skilled in fighting aquatic battles.

Cao Cao realised that not being skilled in naval battles meant fighting in that water was a huge disadvantage, and without these skills he would always be defeated by Zhou Yu. To solve this issue, he employed Cai Mao and Wang Yu who were generals that had experience in naval warfare. Cao Cao's advisor, Zhang Yun, proposed a plan which would not involve a battle, but instead would merely require a manoeuvre. Zhou Yu knew that Cao Cao had employed two generals who were experts in naval battles, which made Zhou Yu feel less powerful. Therefore, Zhang Yun thought that he could propose to Cao Cao to surrender before the battle. Zhang Yun had the advantage of being old school friends with Zhou Yu, and felt he could persuade him to surrender.

Cao Cao had great admiration for Zhang Yun and sent him to the Wu camp to meet with Zhou Yu. Zhou Yu was an intuitive strategist and guessed Zhang Yun's real intent. Even though they were old school friends, Zhou Yu was suspicious of Zhang Yun's arrival, because he had not seen him for many years and wondered why Zhang Yun wanted to meet with him. Zhou Yu knew Zhang Yun was planning something, which led Zhou Yu to apply Strategy Thirty-Three – **The strategy of sowing discord**.

To apply Strategy Thirty-Three, Zhou Yu greeted Zhang Yun in a friendly way. He had delicious food and good wine prepared for their dinner. Zhou Yu's plan was to '*cause discord between Cao Cao and the two generals Cai Mao and Wang Yu*'. Zhou Yu secretly told his employees to prepare two forged letters pretending to be from Cai Mao and Wang Yu. The letters stated that Cai Mao and Wang Yu were planning to assassinate Cao Cao. Zhou Yu left these letters in the open so that Zhang Yun could see them on his desk.

During the dinner Zhou Yu pretended to drink a lot of wine, although he was really filling his glass with water. At the end of the dinner Zhou Yu collapsed on the couch pretending to be drunk. When Zhou Yu had collapsed,

Zhang Yun looked around the quarters of Zhou Yu, which is exactly what Zhou Yu wanted him to do. He found the letters and was very shocked to read that Cai Mao and Wang Yu were planning to assassinate Cao Cao, and after the assassination they would form an alliance with Zhou Yu.

Zhang Yun was '*preoccupied with settling these internal disputes*' and his '*ability to think about the situation was compromised*'. He quickly left Zhou Yu's quarters before Zhou Yu woke up. However, Zhou Yu was only pretending to be asleep. Zhang Yun took the letters with him and left a letter for Zhou Yu saying that he had to return to the Wei camp to attend to an important matter. On his return he read the letters to Cao Cao. Cao Cao was furious, because he felt that the two generals he employed were not to be trusted and was afraid his life was in danger.

He immediately ordered Cai Mao and Wang Yu to be executed. Through the application of Strategy Thirty-Three, Zhou Yu eliminated Cao Cao's most valuable assets, Cai Mao and Wang Yu. Without the skills of Cai Mao and Wang Yu, Cao Cao could not defeat the Zhou Yu army who were skilled in aquatic warfare.

When preparing to apply Strategy Thirty-Three, it is important to conduct detailed research in order to understand what is important to the person whom you are applying this strategy on. The purpose of Strategy Thirty-Three is to disrupt the competitor's environment and to interfere with their ability to think through a situation, because they are so focused on the disruption.

Negotiating with Chinese People

EXAMPLE ONE
Strategy Thirty-Three in action (against you)

In this scenario you export baby milk formula and other dairy products to many countries. You are planning to make China your next export market. However, you are unaware of how to introduce your product to the China market. Firstly, you tried going to your government representatives, who provided you with a list of distributors. As you perceive it would take a lot of time and effort to contact these distributors, in order to find a faster way into the China market you decide to take a different route. You have a Chinese employee who has been working with you for one year, and knows your business well. You decide to use their skills. Through your established contacts you locate a local Chinese company who is doing very well selling milk formula in China. They specialise in milk formula and sell some other Western health-related products. To introduce your product to the China market, you send your Chinese staff member to meet with them, under the pretence that they are a distributor and want to purchase the company's products to export into China.

   This Chinese company deals with many distributors. They have a large network of locations in China through which their milk formula products are distributed. Your intension was not to join their company as one of their distributors, because you were aware you would make more profit doing this alone without using them as a third party. Your Chinese staff member met with the company and asked several questions, with the intension of extracting information from them about their contacts in China.

You were unaware that the Chinese milk formula company had conducted research before this meeting, and they already knew your intention for sending your Chinese staff member to meet with them. With this information they applied Strategy Thirty-Three, by intentionally giving your Chinese staff member the wrong information. The result was that they "*caused discord*" within your company.

They informed your Chinese staff member about three supermarkets, all of which were positioned at the low end of the market, and this information did not prove to be useful. The objective of applying Strategy Thirty-Three was to stop you from positioning yourself as their competitor. As they had done extensive research, they knew that your product was of a high standard, and they also knew that you had very few connections in China to distribute your product.

When your staff member returned to the office with the information, you contacted these places only to find out the market they told you about had a very small distribution channel and was not where you wanted to position your products. You were unhappy because this misinformation wasted your time, and you then questioned your Chinese staff member's skill in getting this information. This '*caused a discord between you and your Chinese staff member*'.

EXAMPLE ONE
Guarding yourself against Strategy Thirty-Three

When first visiting with the government representatives, taking the time to visit the contacts they recommended would have been beneficial, because these contacts had already been vetted by a reliable source. As the Chinese company had conducted extensive research, they were in a good position to apply Strategy Thirty-Three. When they applied Strategy Thirty-Three this was then used to cause friction between you and your Chinese staff member, and therefore take your focus away from the main objective. When sending a staff member to extract information, be aware there is always the risk of being given incorrect information, which is the perfect situation for the application of Strategy Thirty-Three.

EXAMPLE TWO
Strategy Thirty-Three in action (against you)

In this scenario you are an exporter of barley into China. Your barley is high-quality and is used as a key ingredient in one of China's popular beers. During the last five years you have been working with the same distributor, and business is going well. The distributor speaks good English, which is a huge bonus because your Chinese is very limited. As your production relies on weather patterns, in the last year you have had to raise the price of your product because your country has not had favourable weather conditions to grow your product to its maximum quantity and quality.

To keep the standard, you have spent considerable funds purchasing water for irrigation, which has meant you have had to raise your product price. You do not perceive this to be a problem for your Chinese distributor, because they have always talked about your product as being of high-quality, so a slight price rise is, in your opinion, unlikely to make any difference. During this recent price increase you did not realise that your distributor had connected with two other barley growers from other countries, whose prices are not as high as yours.

Your distributor has been '*undermining your product and secretly causing discord between you and the purchaser*'. By applying Strategy Thirty-Three they convince their purchaser that the less expensive products are as good as your product. The distributor's concern was that if they continue to distribute your product, they will lose customers because of the need to increase the cost to make up for the higher price you are charging due to the unfavourable weather conditions in your country.

You only have one distributor, so this situation places you in an insecure position. Your distributor has discussed with the purchaser that the price will not rise if they use either of the two less expensive barley producers. However, if they choose to buy your product the price will inevitably rise. You did not adequately explain to your distributor that this price rise is likely to be temporary due to the unusual weather patterns in your region. Therefore, not fully understanding the situation they presumed this higher price was going to be permanent.

The purchaser of your product has been dealing with your distributor for over a decade and has trust in your distributor's opinion. The result is that the purchaser buys the other two barley products. Even though the quality may be slightly lower, they did not see this as a problem because the distributor advised them that the end consumers would probably not even notice the difference in the taste of the beer. The distributor '*secretly caused a discord between you and the purchaser*'. This resulted in the purchaser having a lower opinion of your company because they perceived your prices had risen too much. As you only had one distributor, this left you with no distribution channel in China.

EXAMPLE TWO
Guarding yourself against Strategy Thirty-Three

Even if your product is in high demand it is likely you will always have a competitor. Therefore, it is important not to become complacent.

The distributor may not have fully understood that your country has weather patterns which can have a positive or negative effect on the growth of your barley. This price rise was likely to be temporary, because if you go back to having favourable weather conditions you will then return to the original price. Like most astute Chinese business people, this distributor was keen to make as much profit as possible, which results in achieving the best deal. It is advisable to have at least two or three distributors, because if something does not work out with one distributor you will have other alternatives. Always remember when dealing with Chinese people that you are dealing with highly sophisticated negotiators.

Key Points when Strategy Thirty-Three is used against you
- Always have more than one distributor when selling into China.
- Remain alert to the possibility that your internal business relationships might be disrupted.
- Assist your distributor in understanding the reasons why there are price changes to your product.

EXAMPLE THREE
Enacting Strategy Thirty-Three

In this scenario you own and operate a chain of upmarket coffee shops in your Western country. You have been running these shops for ten years and have successfully penetrated the high-end market. Your competitive quality is that you have extremely good baristas who understand how to provide excellent customer service. Your plan is to expand your coffee shops into China, and you are aware you will need to locate expert baristas for this expansion to be successful. The key attributes for the baristas you want to employ in China are excellent skills at making coffee, the ability to speak some English, and a high level of understanding about how to provide good customer service.

To locate these people, you contact a market research company in China whose job is to research upmarket coffee shops across China. With this information you then know about your competition in China. The market research company located ten coffee shops with extremely competent baristas. To apply Strategy Thirty-Three, the market research company prepared to '*secretly cause discord between the barista and the coffee shop where they are employed*'.

The research revealed that five of the coffee shops were underpaying their staff, which was the information used to apply Strategy Thirty-Three. The market research company met with the top baristas from these five coffee shops and disclosed to them that they were being underpaid. On hearing this information, the baristas were quite shocked. Because they were '*preoccupied*' with this information, '*their ability to defend their employer was compromised*'.

The market research company then discussed with each of these baristas that a well-established Western chain of high-end coffee shops was in search of expert baristas who know the industry, speak some English, and understand excellent customer service, and let them know that you are prepared to offer these high-quality baristas positions with higher salaries and good working conditions. Strategy Thirty-Three was successfully applied, because you now employ excellent baristas who fit the criteria to successfully expand your business into China.

Negotiating in a Western Environment

EXAMPLE FOUR
Enacting Strategy Thirty-Three

In this scenario you own a small gourmet food business, with products that include fine Mediterranean dips, pesto, salads, and desserts. You supply these products to small delicatessens and cafés. Recently, you have been made aware that a large supermarket in your region is looking to produce and sell similar products under their own brand. To date, you have been the only supplier of these products in your area, and you are aware if a large supermarket begins selling them, people may stop buying from the smaller delicatessens and cafés.

To address this issue, you apply Strategy Thirty-Three, by seeking to supply the supermarket with your products. If they purchase your products, they will have no need to create their own versions. This would be a positive outcome for both parties, because you would profit from such a large deal, and the supermarket would secure an experienced supplier and not have to create a new product range.

To advertise your products, you have a regular stall at local markets and food exhibitions where you offer free samples to customers and potential distributors. To apply Strategy Thirty-Three you get council approval to set up your sample stall outside the supermarket you aim to sell your products to. You advertise by inviting other potential supermarket buyers to try your products, and by doing this '*you are secretly causing discord between the supermarket where you have set up your stall and the other supermarkets*'.

Managers at the supermarket where you have set up your stall also take notice of your products, because they are aware that their competitors have been invited to try samples and are curious to know which supermarkets you will be supplying your products to. You inform them that there are no deals confirmed yet. '*They are preoccupied with this news*', and the manager takes your details to the general manager.

You receive a call from the marketing manager of the supermarket where you set up your stall. They want to discuss the possibility of putting your products into their supermarket. After several months of negotiation, you eventually secure a deal with them. In this way, you have successfully applied Strategy Thirty-Three, with a good outcome for all parties.

Key Points when using Strategy Thirty-Three
- Create opportunities for yourself by disrupting expectations.
- Do your research to ensure you understand your strengths and your competitors' vulnerabilities.
- Create situations and expectations to further your business interests.

The strategy of injuring yourself means *"to injure yourself to appear vulnerable"*

Pretending to be injured has two possible applications. In the first, the enemy is lulled into relaxing his guard since he no longer considers you to be an immediate threat. The second is a way of ingratiating yourself with your enemy by pretending the injury was caused by a mutual enemy.

Emperor Wang Liu was the leader of the prosperous county of Wu. He was highly admired and supported in the leadership of Wu by his son and heir, Qing Li. Wang Liu was excellent in business and generated a lot of wealth for the county of Wu. Wu became extremely rich - so rich that it attracted the attention of Emperor He Lu, who wanted to have this wealth for himself. Emperor He Lu attacked and conquered Wu, killing Wang Liu and many members of his family. Qing Li remained safe, as he was visiting a remote part of Wu at the time of the attack.

Qing Li was devastated by his father's death, and he was furious that He Lu had taken possession of the county of Wu. Qing Li was determined to regain possession of Wu, which meant killing He Lu. Emperor He Lu was equally determined to capture Qing Li, to ensure Qing Li was no longer a threat.

Qing Li was living in close proximity to He Lu, and he had gathered around him many loyal fighters who were also very upset about the killing of his father. To recover Wu, he applied Strategy Thirty-Four - **The strategy of injuring yourself**. Although Qing Li was a physically small man he was a very skilful fighter. To enact Strategy Thirty-Four, Qing Li and a small group of his loyal fighters let themselves be captured by He Lu after an unsuccessful battle. While being captured, Qing Li purposely allowed his right hand to be injured so badly that it needed to be amputated. As Qing Li was maimed in this way, He Lu decided that Qing Li was no longer a threat. By applying Strategy Thirty-Four, He Lu had been *'lulled into relaxing his guard since he no longer considered Qing Li to be a threat'.*

Qing Li pretended to be not disappointed about being beaten by displaying to others he was simply happy to be alive after such an ordeal. The people of Wu were not happy about the leadership of He Lu, and they had trust in Qing Li because he was the son of Wang Liu whom they greatly admired. To apply Strategy Thirty-Four, he announced to the people of Wu that they needed to accept and adjust to the leadership of He Lu, as he was now their new emperor, and that this acceptance would inevitably ensure the ongoing prosperity of Wu. On making this announcement He Lu decided not to kill Qing Li, but rather let him be a low-level advisor for the He Lu Empire. He now saw Qing Li as a small, powerless, disabled man. However, He Lu did not realise that Qing Li was left-handed and therefore the loss of his right hand was not very important, because he was still capable of fighting. Qing Li also had a loyal following who were aware he was applying Strategy Thirty-Four.

He Lu was happy with the way his leadership was going, and Qing Li called Emperor He Lu to show him how he had repaired the city walls. He Lu came outside to view Qing Li's work, with no security protection, because He Lu had *'relaxed his guard as he no longer considered Qing Li to be an immediate threat'*. Qing Li and his loyal fighters attacked He Lu and Qing Li gained control of the county of Wu, which was his father's wish.

When applying Strategy Thirty-Four, it is important that the strategist has strong resources to cope with the injury that they inflict on themselves. The objective of the application of this strategy is for competitors to see no point in putting much effort into continued competition. The strategist is then perceived as no threat and is discarded by their competition.

Negotiating with Chinese People

EXAMPLE ONE
Strategy Thirty-Four in action (against you)

In this scenario you are a reputable real estate company, and one of your largest expenses is marketing. You have a large Chinese clientele, and your specialty is in the residential housing market.

You recognise that cultural issues such as lucky and unlucky numbers are very important to Chinese people, especially when purchasing property. You also recognise that relationships are very important in the Chinese community, so you have focused significant attention on the building of strong *guanxi*. *Guanxi* is about building relationships and is explained in Book Two – *Deceive the*

Dragon: Negotiating to retain power. The only competitor you have in your city is a Chinese real estate agent, who does not spend as much as you do on marketing. You spend a considerable amount on advertising across social media, radio, and print media.

You are involved in one of the largest real estate associations, and you hear from colleagues that your competitor has been having some difficulties, and that these difficulties are consuming their finances. You hear that their offices were flooded which left them with a considerable amount of water damage. The reality was that there was just a small leak, which they exaggerated to seem much larger. They applied Strategy Thirty-Four by '*pretending to be injured*' and announced that they had very limited money left for marketing because their funds had been spent on the repairs caused by the flood.

With this news you were '*lulled into relaxing your guard since you no longer considered them an immediate threat*'. You then decided to stop marketing as much as you had been for the next six months and spent most of your marketing budget on upgrading the computer systems in your office. Your competitor had built up a lot of *guanxi* in the Chinese community, and because many of their friends felt sorry for them, these friends reached out to provide them with marketing resources for a very cheap rate. They then organised events with special Chinese food to thank everyone who had helped them through this difficult time. As you had not done much marketing after you received the news of their difficulties, and therefore many of your Chinese customers did not hear from you as much as they had in the past, they went to your competitor to see what they had to offer. Through these carefully planned actions your competitor gained many of your Chinese clients.

By applying Strategy Thirty-Four, your competitor was able to capture more interest from Chinese customers. As you had decreased your marketing, this left you in a vulnerable position. Your Chinese clients did not hear from you and then went to your competitor.

EXAMPLE ONE
Guarding yourself against Strategy Thirty-Four

In this scenario, because your competitor is a Chinese company, they are likely to have solid connections with the Chinese community. They not only understand what Chinese clients want in a business context, but as this is their own culture they intrinsically understand Chinese people first-hand. As a Western business person, you have had to learn all this information. It is important, no matter what the landscape of your business looks like, that you continue marketing. Even though you have developed a strong relationship with your Chinese customers, this relationship needs to be continually nurtured.

Prior to reducing your marketing budget, it would have been a good idea to analyse the potential problem your competitor was experiencing more closely, and to be aware of the possible application of Strategy Thirty-Four. A significant reduction in marketing for six months leaves the opportunity open for your competitor to step in. A more useful strategy would have been to send them your best wishes and enquire if there was anything you could do to assist them through this crisis.

In this scenario you are an air-conditioning company, in search of high-quality, reasonably priced manufacturers in China. You have always prided yourself on your ethical business standards and want to continue to ensure these standards are maintained. Your local government office introduces you to three manufacturers in China's Guangdong Province. All three companies are in a similar price range, produce high-quality products, offer good customer service, and speak reasonable English.

You hold virtual meetings with all three companies. These companies are competitors and are all in close geographical proximity. When meeting with one of the companies they tell you about an incident they were in the middle of handling, which required them to recall a component. This company, and one of the other three companies you met with, both sourced this faulty component from the same supplier. The company you were communicating with thought that the company who also sourced the faulty component, and who received the component first, should have told them as soon as they knew about this faulty product, which would have saved them a lot of stress. In this communication they were cleverly applying Strategy Thirty-Four. '*They were pretending to be injured*' and saying that this '*injury was caused by a mutual enemy*.'

By applying Strategy Thirty-Four they were presenting the other company in an unethical light. This situation influenced you to make the decision to buy from the company who informed you of this situation, because after being told this, you lost respect for the company who supposedly had prior knowledge of the faulty product.

Through applying Strategy Thirty-Four the company who told you this story gained you as a client, caused their competitor to lose credibility, and gave themselves credibility. After purchasing components off this company for one year, you found out that at the time they recalled these faulty products, they were experiencing financial difficulties. They had applied Strategy Thirty-Four to keep their client base by attempting to demonstrate they were ethical, and to attract new clients and shut out one of their major competitors. In this strategy you were influenced through your ethical and emotional way of operating, which led you to buy off this company without any further research into the reality of the situation. After one year, because of continued financial difficulties, they had to restructure their business and were no longer able to supply you with what you required, which left you without a supplier.

EXAMPLE TWO
Guarding yourself against Strategy Thirty-Four

When dealing with manufacturers in China it is advisable to have more than one manufacturer, because if the situation does not work out with your only manufacturer, this inevitably leaves you without a supplier.

Even if the manufacturer you are communicating with informs you of a situation similar to the company who told you about the faulty product, try to take an objective approach to the situation. In this scenario the manufacturer knew that there was likely to be an emotional reaction, because they were aware that your focus was to ensure your business was ethical.

When you are researching a manufacturer to purchase from, consider that if they are informing you of a situation where they are recalling products, they may be applying Strategy Thirty-Four so that they can gain your sympathy, and hopefully sway you towards purchasing from them. When a company discusses a recall situation, there may be reasons other than just the faulty product behind the discussion. Often the application of Strategy Thirty-Four is used when a business is experiencing financial difficulties where they use this strategy to attract more customers, by demonstrating that their competitor may have treated them unfairly.

Key Points when Strategy Thirty-Four is used against you
- Be alert to the way your emotions may be manipulated.
- Consider why a potential supplier may be unhappy with their competitor.
- Aim to have at least two suppliers.

EXAMPLE THREE
Enacting Strategy Thirty-Four

In this scenario there are two reputable wine companies who are competitors located in the same wine region. One company is owned and operated by a Chinese company and the other is run by Western business people. Both companies get considerable export revenue from China. The Chinese company has a competitive edge because their first language is Chinese, and they understand Chinese business culture first-hand.

There is a Chinese wine purchasing company visiting the wine region. The non-Chinese company are planning ways they can position themselves to be the company of choice for these visiting Chinese clients. Both wine companies use cork stoppers for their wine. The group of Chinese buyers likes this approach because they feel this method demonstrates a more traditional product.

The non-Chinese company had an incident where their cork stoppers contaminated a particular wine variety, and there were two customers who returned their wine purchases. Even though this was not a devastating outcome, the company used this incident to apply Strategy Thirty-Four and 'pretend to be injured'. The application of Strategy Thirty-Four involved recalling all the wine sold that had even the slightest potential to be contaminated. This was an expensive exercise, and the recall situation was well-known in the wine region.

The Chinese-owned wine company 'lulled into relaxing their guard since they no longer considered the other wine company an immediate threat'. When the Chinese buyers visited, the Chinese company thought that they did not have to be as competitive as usual and therefore, to save money, they did the bare minimum to entertain these potential customers.

When the Chinese company visited the Western company, they were very impressed with the way the company had handled the recall of the potentially contaminated wine. The result was that the Chinese company purchased the wine from the Western-owned company because they felt this company demonstrated excellent customer service when they recalled the wine. The Chinese wine producer did not plan any special entertainment for the Chinese buyers because they assumed their competition would lose credibility due to the spoiled wine. By applying Strategy Thirty-Four, the non-Chinese company gained credibility and gained the Chinese buyers as clients.

Negotiating in a Western Environment

Example Four
Enacting Strategy Thirty-Four

In this scenario, you are the owner of a company which supplies car accessories, and one of your main products is car seats for children. You have always prided yourself on your customer service and ethical practices. All your safety accessories undergo multiple checks and abide by quality standards and legal requirements. Many online competitors are emerging, and you are aware that some of your clients now purchase from these businesses. From your research, the online stores lack the personal customer service and the ethical rigour that are the benchmarks of your company.

You apply Strategy Thirty- Four to attract your clientele back from the online stores. When you receive the news that a particular model of a children's car seat needed to be recalled, you use this to your advantage by showcasing your exceptional customer service. Your online competitors have also sold this same children's car seat, and you are confident these online stores will not be very enthusiastic about informing their customers. In fact, their customers may not even receive a notice about the recall.

Your competitors hear about your recall and *'they are lulled into relaxing their guard and no longer consider you to be an immediate threat'*. They perceive this recall will have a negative effect on your reputation, so they reduce the money they spend on their social media advertising, because they assume they will capture the market purely from the implications of this recall situation.

To implement Strategy Thirty- Four *'you pretended to be injured'* by announcing the recall of the children's car seat publicly, and presenting the situation as being worse than it really is. In this announcement you declare that you will not only be recalling the item in question and giving the consumer another product, but you will also be sending them a complimentary car safety accessory to compensate for the inconvenience this recall has caused. Your public communication emphasises how important safety is to your company, and how customers can always rely on you to provide the utmost in quality and safety.

The successful application of Strategy Thirty-Four exposed your competition as unreliable and unethical, and earned your trust and a reputation of being an ethical company working to ensure client safety. Additionally, the positive media attention placed your company in the forefront of people's minds. When people think about infant-safety, they will now automatically think of your company.

Key Points when using Strategy Thirty-Four

- Making a small problem that can be easily rectified look larger than it really is can create goodwill and positive publicity.
- This strategy enables you to show your ethics and values.
- Understand your strengths and your competitors' weaknesses.

The tactic of combining tactics means
"several plans are better than one"

In important matters one should use several strategies applied simultaneously. Keep different plans operating in an overall scheme. In this way, if any one strategy fails you will still have several others to fall back on.

The Prince of Chu was travelling through the Chu region, in proximity to the state of Qi. While on this journey his father died. The prince was very close to his father, and Wang Xu, who was the leader of Qi, was aware that the prince would be experiencing extreme grief. He also knew that he would be taking the throne as the new king of Chu. The Qi army captured the grieving prince and held him prisoner. As the prince would be the newly appointed king, he was anxious to return to his home because the people of Chu would be waiting for him to guide them.

Wang Xu stated that he would release the prince only if he gave the eastern part of Chu territory to the Qi people. The prince felt he had no choice and agreed to this deal. When he returned to his home, he realised that this agreement was a bad idea for the people of Chu, because giving up the eastern part of the Chu territory meant giving up a third of the Chu land.

To save this land, the newly appointed king applied Strategy Thirty-Five. This situation was an important matter for the state of Chu, and the successful application of Strategy Thirty-Five meant that *'in important matters one should use several strategies applied simultaneously. In this way if one strategy failed, he would still have several others to fall back on'*. To apply Strategy Thirty-Five, he discussed the matter individually with three of his best generals, in order to get their advice on how best to deal with this situation.

The first general advised the king to keep his agreement, because in his opinion a noble king stands by their word, and therefore not to honour this agreement would jeopardise his reputation as a newly appointed leader. The second general perceived the deal to be unreasonable, and that the state of Chu would be left powerless if they were to give up this land. He requested permission to fight the state of Qi. The third general advised that this land should not be surrendered, however in his opinion the Chu army were not strong enough to fight the Qi army. So, he advised that the state of Qi should request assistance from a neighbouring territory who had a strong army, in order to help them fight for the land.

To apply Strategy Thirty-Five – **The tactic of combining tactics,** the king accepted the advice from all three generals because he wanted to *'keep different plans operating in the overall scheme'*. The first general met with Wang Xu to surrender the land as originally agreed. The king then instructed the second general to gather the Chu army and defend the land. Then the king sent the third general to the neighbouring territory to ask for their help in fighting for the land. All these plans were simultaneously put into action, which left the state of Qi in confusion.

Amidst this confusion, Wang Xu instructed his troops to launch an attack on the state of Chu. When the Qi army arrived in the Chu territory ready to commence a battle against the State of Chu, the third general arrived just behind them and was escorted by the troops of the neighbouring territory who were an experienced army and outnumbered the Qi army. This resulted in Wang Xu feeling he was in a no-win position, so he called off the battle and the king of Chu was able to keep the land.

The application of Strategy Thirty-Five provides the strategist with more flexibility, making it difficult for their opponent to understand what is going on.

Negotiating with Chinese People

EXAMPLE ONE
Strategy Thirty-Five in action (against you)

In this scenario you are an abalone grower, and you have heard from several business contacts that in China's upmarket restaurants abalone are very popular. Your government office has connected you with a reputable Chinese distributor whose business is in a city thirty minutes by plane from where you live.

One of your close business contacts deals with this Chinese company and has informed you they are ethical, speak very good English, are experienced negotiators, and clever business people. Even though you have not had any business dealings with Chinese business people, you feel confident you can deal with these Chinese distributors. The Chinese company invite you to their offices, and on your arrival they demonstrate great hospitality by meeting you at the airport.

On the way to your hotel the driver is very friendly and politely asks you when you are leaving to fly back home. You arrived on a Tuesday, and casually answer the driver telling them that your plane departs on the following Thursday morning at 10am. As you have limited experience with Chinese business culture, you did not realise by answering in this way you have provided them with the opportunity for Strategy Four – **Wait leisurely for an exhausted enemy** to be applied on you. Strategy Four is discussed in Book One – *Tame the Tiger: Negotiating from a position of power*. To apply Strategy Four the driver will relay the information regarding your departure time to the Chinese company, which means the Chinese company will know when you are leaving and will endeavour to exhaust you the night before you leave. The assumption is that you will then be too tired to put very much energy into a meeting before you board your plane, which means they will have the upper hand on issues such as pricing.

On the Tuesday evening you are taken out for dinner. As the representatives of the company are extremely friendly you are feeling good about conducting business with them and perceive the next couple of days will go smoothly. On the Wednesday you meet at their office, and your plan is to commence the discussions about pricing. When you start talking about pricing, they apply Strategy Six – **Make a noise in the East and attack in the West** from Book One – *Tame the Tiger: Negotiating from a position of power.* They do this by manoeuvring the discussion away from the topic of price. Instead, they discuss issues such as size, weight, delivery dates, and other logistics regarding the purchasing of your abalone. As the Chinese company knows that you must leave the next morning, they endeavour to keep you up very late on the Wednesday night by taking you out and creating a situation where it is impossible for you to say no to their hospitality.

In a tired state of mind, caused by the ramifications of the entertainment of the night before, you meet with the Chinese company on the Thursday morning at 7am. They convey to you that they are happy with what you are offering, however before fixing prices they would like to have further discussions and invite you to return in two weeks. They apply Strategy Fifteen – **Lure the tiger down the mountain** from Book Three – *Lure the Tiger: Negotiating in confronting circumstances.* Their request is for this meeting to be held in their other premises, because they want to show you these offices. However, this location is in a different city. As you have already used resources to visit them, they offer to pay your accommodation for this next visit. As this is a city that you are not familiar with, you are inevitably taken out of your comfort zone, which places them in a position of control. In this situation several strategies have been played out, leaving you vulnerable.

Example One
Guarding yourself against Strategy Thirty-Five

Always keep in mind that most Chinese people are expert negotiators. Even when you have a good understanding of business in the Western business environment, these Western business skills are not likely to be transferable into the Chinese business world. When a Chinese person picks you up at the airport and asks you when you are leaving it is highly likely they are applying Strategy Four – **Wait leisurely for an exhausted enemy**. To guard yourself against Strategy Four it is important to answer this question in a vague manner, simply by stating that you have not yet confirmed your flight.

To deal with Strategy Six – **Make a noise in the East and attack in the West**, you need to keep the strategist on track, by continuing to bring the conversation back to what you want to discuss. In this scenario the plan was to discuss prices, so when Strategy Six was applied the Chinese company continued to veer around the topic of price by discussing every other issue except the price.

When meeting with the Chinese company on the Thursday morning they applied Strategy Fifteen – **Lure the tiger down the mountain**. Chinese business people are likely to try to find ways to negotiate on their own territory, because this means they will inevitably have more control. To guard yourself against Strategy Fifteen you need to push back by suggesting having these discussions at your office. A possible way around this would be to invite them to visit the abalone farm and tell them your reason for this invitation is that you would like them to see your operations in action. This then means they will be on your territory and you have more control.

EXAMPLE TWO
Strategy Thirty-Five in action (against you)

You have a unique building material that is used for walls in residential housing. The material's attributes are that it is easy to paint and is long lasting. One of your contacts informed you of a manufacturer in China that is likely to be able to make your product for a cost-effective price. You contact this company and send them photographs and other specifications outlining what you require. They are confident they can make this for you, and you visit their manufacturing plant in China.

You are met at the airport, which pleases you because this is your first time visiting China. You check into your hotel while the driver waits for you in the hotel lobby, and you are then escorted to a restaurant. Everything at the restaurant seems very non-threating, and they have even organised for beer that is produced in your country to be on the dinner table, which makes you feel very at home. They are applying Strategy One – **Fool the emperor to cross the sea** from Book One – *Tame the Tiger: Negotiating from a position of power*. This is where you are placed in an environment constructed in such a way that you feel comfortable, because things are made to feel familiar.

During the dinner conversation you are asked about pricing, and because you feel you are in a non-threatening environment you tell them your bottom price, which leaves no room for bargaining. In your mind the business commences the next day. You did not realise that in the Chinese business environment the moment you meet the Chinese business person is when the business begins.

Most of the group speak no English and they offer to provide you with an interpreter, which you gratefully accept. They are applying Strategy Thirty – **Exchange the role of guest for that of host**, from Book Five – *Endure the Tiger: Negotiating to gain ground*. This is where the interpreter crosses boundaries they should not and moves into a position of power.

When you walk into the meeting the head person of the group does not communicate with you, which confuses you. They are applying Strategy Three – **Murder with a borrowed knife**, from Book One – *Tame the Tiger: Negotiating from a position of power*. You did not realise the head person in Chinese business culture says the least, and it is the second most senior person who is the most appropriate person to communicate with. You are now in the position where you are in a foreign country, you have told the company a price that you are not happy with, the interpreter has overridden you, and you are trying to communicate with the person who will provide you with the least answers. In this situation the Chinese company have applied Strategy Thirty-Five because '*in this matter if one strategy fails, they still have other strategies to fall back on.*'

Guarding yourself against Strategy Thirty-Five

When doing business with Chinese people it is essential that you have some understanding of the 36 Strategies. Strategy One – **Fool the emperor to cross the Sea** was applied when you felt relaxed and comfortable in the Chinese business environment. Whenever you feel comfortable and relaxed, remember that you need to be on guard and therefore think clearly about what you say. This does not mean you need to be rigid, it simply means you need to be aware. Negotiation commences when you first meet your Chinese counterparts. Unlike Western culture where negotiation is a component of the business deal, in the Chinese business environment, negotiation is in every facet of the business. Therefore, whatever you say outside any formal meetings will be considered a significant part of the negotiation.

Organising your own interpreter will prevent your Chinese contact from applying Strategy Thirty – **Exchange the role of guest for that of host**. In professional settings interpreters are not permitted to have any input into meetings, rather only to relay what you need to say.

Hierarchy is not as imbedded in Western culture as it is in Chinese culture, so it is easy for a Western person to expect to communicate directly with the head of a company. When you attend a Chinese meeting, expect that Strategy Three – **Murder with a borrowed knife** is always in action.

Key Points when Strategy Thirty-Five is used against you
- Anticipate that several strategies will be enacted on you.
- Plan how you will manage to remain in charge of any negotiation.
- Remember every part of communication contributes to the negotiation.

Example Three
Enacting Strategy Thirty-Five

In this scenario you have designed a piece of software that uses voice technology to survey customers about the product they have purchased. You envisage China as a lucrative market for your product. Chinese people are likely to feel non-threatened when using voice technology to provide their opinion because they not only find form filling tedious, but there is also a possibility that these written feedback forms can cause a Chinese person 'loss of face'. Chinese people may feel embarrassed if the person who is collecting the survey data has access to their personal opinions. This software is fully automated and there is no possibility of an individual person listening to the feedback, as everything is collated and de-identified automatically.

To locate Chinese buyers for your software, you visit China and attend three networking functions where you meet several Chinese business people who show interest in your product. Even though you feel most of these companies will not be suitable buyers for your product you treat them as if you are very interested in having them purchase your software. To do this you apply Strategy Ten - **Hide your dagger behind a smile,** which is described in Book Two – *Deceive the Dragon: Negotiation to retain power*. This is where you tell each of the Chinese businesses you are interested in doing business with them, even though you may not be. The reason for this response is to develop *guanxi*.

After talking with many Chinese companies, you choose three companies that you think may be suitable for you to deal with. When meeting with each of these three companies, you apply Strategy Twenty-Seven – **Feign madness but keep your balance**, from Book Five – *Endure the Tiger: Negotiating to gain ground*. You do this by not disclosing your knowledge, and instead providing them the space to do most of the talking. In this way you can analyse whether or not they have the expertise that is required to successfully use your software product. From these three companies you choose two companies to purchase your software. One company runs educational online courses to train aged care workers, and the other company manufactures pet accessories for the Chinese market.

After dealing with these companies for six months you are aware the training organisation has a key staff member who does not use the software to its greatest capacity. You do not want to approach this person directly as this would cause 'loss of face'. So, you apply Strategy Twenty-Six – **Point at the mulberry but curse the locust tree** from Book Five – *Endure the Tiger: Negotiating to gain ground*, which means to indirectly communicate an issue. To do this you communicate with the person in question and say that you think someone else in another company is using the software incorrectly. By describing the incorrect use of the software, they then recognise that they are the person in question and learn to use the software correctly without 'losing face'.

Three strategies have been successfully used to sell this software product in China, analyse the capacity of potential buyers, and address issues without causing 'loss of face'. *'In this way if any one strategy fails you will still have several others to fall back on'.*

Negotiating in a Western Environment

Example Four
Enacting Strategy Thirty-Five

In this scenario you want to reignite the live-music scene in your local community. At the time you were planning to do this, the media announce that a prominent singer who once played in your local area has died unexpectedly. The community really admired this singer, and the tragedy has sparked a great deal of nostalgia. As you want to organise a live-music event you take advantage of the situation by applying Strategy Five – **Loot a burning house** from Book One – *Tame the Tiger: Negotiating from a position of power.* Strategy Five is applied when you want to capitalise on a crisis.

Your research reveals that live music was very popular in the 1980's. Also, in the 1980's there was a banner often used which read 'These are the Days'. As these are words that many people in the community can relate to, instead of introducing a new banner to advertise the live music event, you apply Strategy Fourteen – **Borrow a corpse to raise the spirit** from Book Three – *Lure the Tiger: Negotiating in confronting circumstances,* by using the words on the original banner. Strategy Fourteen is used to reinterpret something from the past. Your aim is to plan an event that will appeal to the age group who relate to the words on the banner from the 1980's. Even if a younger community do not relate to these words on the banner, their parents are likely to enjoy introducing this piece of history to their children and may share stories about the music scene in the 1980s.

As people commence buying tickets you use Strategy Twelve – **Seize the opportunity to lead a sheep away** from Book Two – *Deceive the Dragon: Negotiating to retain power.* When applying Strategy Twelve the strategist takes every possible opportunity, which in this situation means engaging as many people as possible to be involved in this event. With this in minds, you ask friends, family, and colleagues to spread the word about the event. You also to approach local celebrities and artists and ask them to participate, and they are happy to do so because they perceive this as great advertising.

By using several strategies, you have gained interest from all age groups to revive a live-music scene. For the successful application of Strategy Thirty-Five *'One should use several strategies applied simultaneously, and keep different plans operating in an overall scheme'.*

Key Points when using Strategy Thirty-Five

- Realise that there will be several strategies that you can use within any negotiation.
- Be mindful about how you will approach every business interaction.
- Be flexible when doing business, and find many avenues to apply the appropriate strategies.

If all else fails, retreat means *"when you run away quietly you can always make a comeback"*

If it becomes obvious that your current course of action will lead to defeat, then retreat and regroup. When your side is losing there are only three choices remaining: surrender, compromise, or escape. Surrender is complete defeat, compromise is half defeat, but escape is not defeat. As long as you are not defeated, you still have a chance.

*E*mperor Hui Dao was the leader for many years during the Ming Dynasty. There was a lot of animosity during his leadership because his uncles continually threatened to kill him and take the throne. He had no choice but to dispose of these uncles, as they were a threat to the throne. However, there was one uncle, the Prince of Yan, whom he was unable to kill. The Prince of Yan wanted to take the throne, and in order to do this his army besieged the city of Nanjing, where the emperor resided.

Emperor Hui Dao was extremely frightened, to the point where he considered taking his own life. An old family friend who had been close to the late Emperor Hong Wu, who was Emperor Hui Dao's grandfather, stopped Hui Dao from taking his own life. Hong Wu had left a chest in his friend's care, giving directions that should any major crisis happen to his grandson which threatened the dynasty, his grandson must open this chest.

The family friend assisted Hui Dao in applying Strategy Thirty-Six – **If all else fails, retreat** by giving Emperor Hui Dao the chest and instructing him to open it. As Emperor Hui Dao was aware, he was in a desperate situation and he considered there were '*only three choices remaining which were surrender, compromise, or escape*'. He knew that '*escape was not defeat*', and '*as long as you are not defeated you still have a chance*'. He opened the chest to discover it contained the robes of a Buddhist monk and a razor. After shaving his head, he donned the robes and fled the palace through a secret tunnel to a Buddhist monastery where he lived in disguise for many years.

Shortly after he fled to the monastery, the Nanjing palace was burnt down by the Prince of Yan's troops, and it was assumed that Emperor Hui Dao had died in the fire. After Hui Dao had left, the Ming Dynasty was under the leadership of Emperor Wang Jing, who was the leader for two decades. Wang Jing had great respect for the past leadership of Emperor Hui Dao.

One day, a monk arrived in Nanjing claiming he had seen Hui Dao in a monastery. Everyone in Nanjing was curious. To see if the story was true Emperor Wang Jing arranged for an investigation into the monastery. The investigators found Hui Dao practicing as a Buddhist priest. Emperor Wang Jing then invited Hui Dao to return to Nanjing to live out the rest of his life as a guest at the palace.

By applying Strategy Thirty-Six Hui Dao had been able to '*retreat and regroup*' and was not defeated, which enabled him to return to the palace after many years. The skill in applying Strategy Thirty-Six is knowing the right time to escape, so that you can always come back.

Negotiating with Chinese People

EXAMPLE ONE
Strategy Thirty-Six in action (against you)

In this scenario your company has developed robotic technology that is used for physical rehabilitation. The customer group are post-accident victims. These robotic devices help customers achieve more movement through intensive repetitive actions, which are tiring for human physical therapists to conduct on their patients.

You want to export to China and require a reputable Chinese business partner who has strong connections to government rehabilitation hospitals and aged care facilities. Your government office located three companies. You held virtual meetings with all three companies and discovered they are all interested in your product. However, one company really stood out and you continue to have regular communication with this potential Chinese business partner. You were almost ready to conduct the deal with them, although you still wanted some information about their client base.

They were unclear with you and you did not realise they were trying to stall the process of answering your enquiries as they had not fully developed the *guanxi* needed to successfully grow the business. The Chinese company stopped contacting you, which did not make any sense because generally in a Western business context, when a business person is not capable or does not want to conduct business they tell you up front.

In this situation they applied Strategy Thirty-Six, so they could '*retreat and regroup*' and come back to you when they had acquired adequate resources. After six months of very little communication, you decided to contact one of the other two companies that your local government office had previously introduced. They were not your first choice, but you were keen to commence your China business. After one year, much to your surprise, the first company contacted you and explained that they were well equipped to handle and develop the business, and keen to begin working with you. At this point you had used up all your resources on the company you had chosen to work with and could no longer accommodate your first choice.

EXAMPLE ONE
Guarding yourself against Strategy Thirty-Six

Even when Western business people are experienced in working with Chinese business people, they often do not fully understand Chinese business culture. One of the key communication differences in the Western business environment is that if you are unable to conduct business, you will probably say this upfront. In the Chinese business environment, if someone is interested in doing business with you and they stop contacting you, they are likely to be applying Strategy Thirty-Six. By applying Strategy Thirty-Six they have left the door open and will get back in contact with you when they are fully equipped to conduct business with you.

If you exhaust all your resources on the company that is your second choice, then there is no space left for the company that would have been your first choice to come back into your business environment. Leaving some resources for a future partnership with your preferred Chinese business partner is wise.

EXAMPLE TWO
Strategy Thirty-Six in action (against you)

In this scenario you work as a high-level public servant in an international business department for your local government. For over a decade your city has had a sister city relationship with Qingdao, which is in China's Shandong province. Sister city relationships are driven by government-to-government connections, and from this relationship business deals are potentially developed. In a Chinese context, a sister city relationship is considered as important as the relationship you have with a close family member.

A high-profile Chinese delegation representing this sister city visited your city. They stayed for one week, during which time they had several meetings with government departments and private sector businesses. Everyone who was involved in these meetings was very excited about the potential of business deals with China. During their visit, many Memorandums of Understanding (MOU) were signed. Signing a MOU is common practice for Chinese people before they sign a contract. Although an MOU is not legally binding it is a great place to start building business relationships with Chinese business people.

After the Chinese delegation returned to China you did not hear anything from them for two months. You were not aware that they were waiting for their government to meet to discuss China's next five-year plan. As this five-year plan directs China as to what sectors to invest in, and therefore what foreign entities to conduct business with, it was only after this meeting that they were able to make any decisions. By not contacting you they were applying Strategy Thirty-Six, because they wanted to '*retreat and regroup*'.

During this two-month period of no communication from China you were being pressured by the businesses and your government's offices as to when you would be hearing from these contacts in China. Under pressure, you decided to move forward by contacting business people in other countries in the Asian region, whom you had previously developed relationships with. These business opportunities were quickly taken up by businesses in these other countries. After three months, the Chinese contacts who had visited your city contact you and inform you of the businesses they would like to deal with.

As business deals were already signed with representatives in other countries in the Asia region, you were placed in the embarrassing situation of having to explain to your Chinese contacts that the businesses they met with are now conducting business with their neighbours in the Asia region, who are their competitors. This situation put them in second place, displayed your ignorance of the timing and significance of China's five-year plan, and showed disrespect towards the sister city relationship.

EXAMPLE TWO
Guarding yourself against Strategy Thirty-Six

When dealing with China it is crucial to understand and keep up with significant government meetings, because government meetings in China are the basis for decision making with regards to what industry sectors China will focus on. If your actions demonstrate that you know nothing about these important meetings, then your Chinese contacts are likely to think you have little interest in their country. Knowing the reason as to why their decision to secure deals was taking longer than expected, you could have then advised your government colleagues and private businesses that this was normal behaviour, and therefore they needed to be patient. By going to other countries in the Asian region, who are your Chinese contact's competitors, you push your Chinese contacts into second place.

Key Points when Strategy Thirty-Six is used against you

- Building *guanxi* takes time and money, so be patient if your investment with your Chinese partner is taking time.
- Recognise that silence from your Chinese contact may simply mean that they are still building the necessary *guanxi*, or have some other constraint, and that they are likely to get back to you.
- Do your research and understand the reasons China makes decisions.

Example Three
Enacting Strategy Thirty-Six

In this situation you are a reputable agricultural company who has developed a fertiliser product which is environmentally friendly and quickly brings depleted farmland back to a healthy farming condition. Your research demonstrates that the overuse of farmland is a growing concern in rural China because it results in the end product being low in nutrients.

Your local government office informs you that they have had an enquiry from the provincial government in Western China's Gansu Province. The Gansu local government is interested in purchasing your product. Following this enquiry, you send samples of your fertiliser to the contact in Gansu Province. After a couple of weeks of receiving your samples, they request a very large order of your fertiliser. Although this request is something you were expecting, the size of the order is astounding. During the ten years you have been conducting business internationally, you have never been asked for an order this large. You are concerned that your company does not have the resources to fulfil such a huge order. However, you do not want to lose this large customer, so to solve this issue you applied Strategy Thirty-Six.

From the excellent response you have had from your China contacts you perceive they are likely to want to purchase this product for other rural locations in China, besides Gansu Province. You were aware that because there is a huge need for your product in China, large orders are likely to be a common occurrence. *'It has become obvious that the current course of action,'* that you would normally apply, which is to be up front and state you cannot supply this large quantity, would probably lead to losing this significant contract. To apply Strategy Thirty-Six, you *'retreat and regroup'*. By halting the communication with your Chinese contacts for two months, you give yourself the time to organise the infrastructure which is needed to manage these large orders. After two months, you reconnect with your China customers, ready to manage large orders from all customers in China.

Negotiating in a Western Environment

EXAMPLE FOUR
Enacting Strategy Thirty-Six

In this scenario you have been working for many years in a student advisory role at a university. The role is to liaise with students and university staff. When you initially commenced this role, your job involved communicating with many people and assisting with their queries. Recently, the university has had a major restructure, which meant your job tasks shifted from servicing a school of 1,000 staff and students, to servicing five schools within the university. This meant that you would be the front person for enquiries for a total of 5,000 staff and students. Even though your workload dramatically increased, your pay remained the same. As you had a significantly larger workload, the job was beginning to drain your energy. While all of these changes were happening, the manager requested your assistance on a large project.

After analysing this situation, you realise you were faced with three choices, which were 'to surrender, compromise, or retreat'. If you 'surrender' to the manager, this meant choosing to continue with your current workload and, in addition, take on the new project, which would inevitably result in complete exhaustion. The 'compromise' option did not suit you because this would mean requesting to decrease your hours to part time. 'Retreat' was your best option. So, to deal with this situation you applied Strategy Thirty-Six by accepting another job where the workload was manageable, and the pay was fair.

Even though you left the university job to a position where you would be more valued and not overworked, it is possible that circumstances may change at the university. As you have a good reputation in the university workplace environment, you are quite convinced you could return to working there if you wished. 'As long as you are not defeated, you still have a chance', therefore there is always the chance to return.

Key Points when using Strategy Thirty-Six
- Taking your time to respond within a negotiation enables you to ensure you can get necessary preparation completed.
- There is no dishonour in walking away from an impossible situation, and this does not mean you cannot return.
- To retreat from a situation means you can always come back.

Your Next Steps

Having just finished reading *Flee the Dragon*, here are some suggestions for your next steps:

- Now I can plan my approach when I am negotiating in any situation.
- The 36 Strategies will help me when communicating with Chinese people.
- I will share this knowledge with my colleagues.
- I want to read *The Dao of Negotiation* series. I'll find them at **www.leoniemckeon.com**
- I will contact Leonie to:
  - Help me think completely differently about my business development challenges.
  - Deliver a presentation for my next conference or other event.
  - Deliver 36 Strategies workshops to my team.
- Because **Pronounce Mandarin - The Easy Way** is perfect for beginners, I will learn how to correctly pronounce Chinese names and some useful Mandarin Chinese words and phrases via **www.pronouncemandarin.com**

Go to **www.leoniemckeon.com** for more information about the 36 Strategies. Leonie has several informative videos and blogs to help you further your understanding of how to negotiate in any business environment.

WHAT PEOPLE SAY ABOUT WORKING
WITH LEONIE MCKEON

BEC HARDY WINES

"I can't tell you how much you have given our family, and me personally, through your insights about the 36 Chinese Strategies. Understanding how the 36 Chinese Strategies are applied in Chinese business culture was the lightbulb moment which has led to such revenue growth, opportunities and personal growth. This has been one of the great, exciting professional and personal journeys and achievements of my life. Thanks again."

Richard Dolan, Joint Managing Director

HATCH, Western Australia

"Anyone who has the pleasure of having dealings with China and the Chinese will find Leonie's 36 Chinese Strategies workshops invaluable. The workshops were eye-opening and had the right amount of humour and personal stories to more than keep our attention."

Denis Pesci, PDG Hub Director, Western Australia

Fletcher Building

"From a personal perspective, Leonie was instrumental to our Chinese cultural program developed for the Super Retail Group. The target audience for the workshop was our Management and Leaders from Logistics, Marketing and Category. In organising the program for the team, I found Leonie incredibly resourceful, totally understood the brief and built value-add to the program. Often you don't know what you don't know so great to have a Subject Matter Expert to guide and shape a very successful program."

Shirley Brown, Capability Development Manager –
Australian Distribution

Australian American Fulbright Commission

"The Art of Negotiation – 36 Strategies derived from 'The Art of War' workshop delivered by Leonie at the Australian Institute of Company Directors (AICD) challenged conventional thinking."

Peter de Cure, Chairman, Australian American Fulbright Commission

Kmart

"The training that Leonie provided to our team was excellent. The program was practical, delivered with context, and opened the team members' minds to learning more about how to do better business in China. I have no doubt that what we have learned will be applied and will provide great outcomes for our business. Leonie has also provided a great personal development opportunity for members of our team."

Matthew Webber, International Supply Chain Manager

The Dao of Negotiation
The Path between Eastern Strategies and Western Minds

		Strategy Number
Book One – *Tame the Tiger*	Advantageous Strategies	1, 2, 3, 4, 5, 6
Book Two – *Deceive the Dragon*	Opportunistic Strategies	7, 8, 9, 10, 11, 12,
Book Three – *Lure the Tiger*	Strategies for Attack	13, 14, 15, 16, 17, 18
Book Four – *Bewilder the Dragon*	Confusion Strategies	19, 20, 21, 22, 23, 24
Book Five – *Endure the Tiger*	Strategies for Gaining Ground	25, 26, 27, 28, 29, 30
Book Six – *Flee the Dragon*	Strategies for Desperate Situations	31, 32, 33, 34, 35, 36

The Dao of Negotiation:
The Path between Eastern Strategies and Western Minds

by Leonie McKeon

More Control, More Success, More Wins!

Based on *The Art of War*, *The Dao of Negotiation* series unmask the 36 Strategies used in Chinese culture and business.

This incredible series of 6 books provide invaluable tips for any business person looking to improve their overall negotiation skills, as well as become better at negotiating with Chinese People.

Discover how you can use this ancient wisdom for more business success.

www.leoniemckeon.com

www.ingramcontent.com/pod-product-compliance
Lightning Source LLC
Chambersburg PA
CBHW072248210326
41458CB00073B/836